WINNING HABITS

Foreword by Pastor E.A.ADEBOYE

PETER AMENKHIENAN

Another Bestseller from the Author of Achieving Success

PRAISE FOR WINNING HABITS

"Winning or Losing in the affairs of life is a matter of habits. Everyone wants to be a success and a winner in all realms of life. We all grew up with dreams and visions within our inner man. Our dreams were to be the best we could be, but not everyone reaches that level. Some do, but majority do not. Winning Habits is a book that is meant to teach us how to succeed and be perpetual winners. Reading this book alone will not produce the necessary results. But digesting the gems and putting them to practice will make winners out of us."

- E. A. Odeyemi, State Pastor, Headquaters State I, R.C.C.G. and General Secretary Christ the Redeemers Ministries, Lagos. Nigeria.
"Success in life is tied to your habit. Your rising to stardom solely depend on your being consistent and resilient. The gems in this book have divine catalysts that will activate your speed to your destiny.
Pastor Amenkhienan's deep revelation of winning habits are boosters to help you arrive at your destination. Read on."

- J. F. Odesola State Pastor, Ogun State I R. C. C.G and National Travelling Secretary Christ the Redeemers Ministries Lagos. Nigeria.

"This book is another precious gem from a proven author. Read it and keep it. Don't give it out. You will always need to refer to it because winners are well informed... the extent of divine transformation experienced depends on the amount of divine information at one's disposal. This is divine information."

- Dr. Omadeli Boyo, MD. Pinecrest Hospitals, Lagos. Nigeria.

"Success in any field is not an accident. This book combines a wealth of material from the life's of successful people with tremendous revelations of God's word, to help direct our thinking for a life of a cornucopia of economic and spiritual success. Read it and Win."

- *Pastor **Chris Oyakhilome***, *President Believers LoveWorld Ministries a.k.a Christ Embassy, Lagos, Nigeria.*

"Pastor Peter Amenkhienan has spelt out in his books "Winning Habits" the ingredients of true success. It is recommended for those who desire to leave their mark on the sand of time."

- ***E. A. Adeboye***, *General Overseer The Redeemed Christian Church of God*

DEDICATION

To Chief & Mrs George Apa Amenkhienan, my wonderful parents who taught me hardwork and personal integrity early in life. Members of the Redeemed Christain Church of God, Abundant Life family Ota, whose desire for balanced Spiritual diet inspires me to dig deep into the Word all the time.

ACKNOWLEDGEMENT

My greatest thanks goes to my father in the Lord, Pastor E. A. Adeboye, Who found time out of his busy schedule to read the manuscript and write the foreword. I wish to also acknowledge the contributions of Rev. Chris Oyakhilome, Pastor E. A Odeyemi, Pastor J. F. Odesola and Dr Omadeli Boyo. The encouragement received from my bosom friends especially my wife Asst. Pastor Sola Amenkhienan, Lt. Col. D. A. Itodo, Asst. Pastor Bosun Qgunro is worthy of note. This book would not have become a reality, but for the sacrificial work of Asst. Pastor Bisi Akande, Deacon Spencer Elugbe, Tunde Dopemu, Lolade Osunlabu, Funmi Afelumo and my book project partners. To them all I express my gratitude. Above all, I acknowledge God the Holy Spirit, my helper and comforter who gave me inspiration to write this book.

CONTENTS

FOREWORD

An individual without a vision is like a piece of wood adrift in a mighty ocean, tossed to and fro by the tempestuous Waves, with no goal and no specific destination.

A man of vision is however a man of purpose, with an understanding of his goal and the means to achieving it. But as wonderful as it is to have a vision, some habits formed in an individual's life can scuttle visions and reduce the visioner to nothing but a rabble-rouser with so much fuss but with little or no results to show for it.

Since true success is measured in lasting terms, the individual who would be considered a Winner must possess the qualities to make the successful venture to subsist and to endure.

Peter Amenkhienan has spelt out in his book **"Winning Habits"** the ingredients of true success. It is recommended for those who desire to leave their mark on the sands of time.

PASTOR E.A. ADEBOYE
General Overseer
The Redeemed Christian Church of God Worldwide

INTRODUCTION

Every Winner I have known, has strong productive habits that are far reaching and result oriented. Godly habits that are carefully formed through deliberate efforts. These Winners are men with character and strong will. They hold on stubbornly to what they believe in. They are quick to tap from their God given abilities.

Even in unfavorable conditions they carry their own Weather along with them. They attract attention through their vision. They are never to be found in the unemployment market, there is something in demand about them. Their strongest appeal is the acceptability and marketability of their good character. Little wonder then that they sit in high places from Where they rule and reign in their generation. Diligence is their Watchword.

> *"Seest thou a man diligent in his business? he Shall stand before kings; he shall not stand before mean men."*
> *- Prov. 22:29*

These habits are found in the lives of our forefathers in the faith: Abraham, Isaac, Jacob, Joseph, Jephthah, David, Peter, Paul, Martin Luther and John Wesley.

A closer look into the lives of the end-time kingdom generals shows that these habits are clearly in operation in their daily routine. Men like Billy Graham, Paul Youngi Cho, Pastor E.A. Adeboye, the late Arch Bishop B.A. Idahosa, Oral Roberts, T.L. Osborne, Morris Cerrulo, Bishop David Oyedepo, T.D. Jakes and many others.

These Winners fear no failure, they fly when others faint. Courage is never in Want wherever they operate. They fight with current information. Knowledge is their weapon of Warfare. Nothing stops them. The supernatural ability of turning obstacles into miracles is found in them.

This book has therefore, packaged some of these habits for us to study and imbibe. No man escapes loosing without them. So never allow them depart from your life. Inculcate them day and night and you'll be a shining star in this dark world.

WINNING HABITS

PETER AMENKHIENAN

CHAPTER 1

Winners Live With A Positive Attitude

Your attitude will either make a palace or a prison for you, out of this world. Attitude is a manner of acting, or behavior that shows ones inward thoughts or feelings. It is either positive or negative. Right or wrong. It is very difficult to conceal the real attitude. If a person's attitude is not clear in behavior, the actions and reactions viz-a-viz the result of actions will show clearly what his attitude is.

Everyone has God given abilities. When a person's attitude enhances his ability he becomes unstoppable in any endeavor. Obstacles, turn to miracles. That is why a right attitude is the greatest determinant of high performance in life. No wonder someone said attitude is everything.

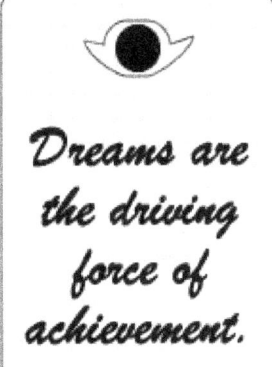

Dreams are the driving force of achievement.

The person with a positive attitude, wins even before he starts, while the person with a negative attitude quits before he starts.

Everyone can start a marathon race, but only the person with the right attitude finishes the race. So your success or failure in life hinges on your attitude.

"Your attitude should be the kind that was shown us by

Jesus Christ"
- Phillipians 2:5 (TLB)

Anyone with a right attitude never waits for help from others before rising to work. He's willing to take the first step. He changes
and charges positively towards any event before expecting things
to change for good. If this attitude is in you, you will never be
found stunted in growth in this land of stunning riches.

People with a wrong attitude to life are controlled by circumstances. They are in fact creatures of circumstance. But not so
when you have the right attitude. Circumstances come under your
perfect control. So, for things to be right, your attitude must be
right.

> *"When a man is gloomy, everything seems to go wrong;*
> *when he's cheerful, everything seems right"*
> *- Proverbs 15:15 (TLB)*

Winners are those who develop right perspective to life. They be-
lieve that success is not limited to one particular country or town.
That success can be obtained anywhere. They have the right spirit.
And right spirit produces right ideas, thoughts and action.

> *"Create in me a clean heart, O God; and renew a right spirit*
> *within me"*
> *- Ps. 51:10*

Living in hell or heaven here on earth depends entirely on your attitude to life. Nothing reasonable is ever achieved with a negative
attitude. Only positive attitude towards life enables you think correctly, see correctly, talk correctly and act correctly.

Godliness And Attitude

> *"But Godliness with contentment is great gain"*
> *- I Timothy 6:6*

Godliness will greatly profit any man desiring to sail through life with a positive attitude. Godliness is showing obedience to God and his divine laws by living a holy, devoured and pious life. You need not be a Pastor, Priest and Bishop before you can be godly. Godliness is a strong requirement for a steady victorious life.

The positive attitude of the three Hebrew children; Shadrach, Meshach and Abednego who made history by defying the burning fiery furnace of Babylon was greatly enhanced by godliness. In other words, to be able to overcome the fiery problems of life godliness is required. Godliness breeds courage, persistency and determination which are the needed ingredients for a positive attitude. Courage and faith will cure fear during crisis.

Determination will ensure distinction in success, while persistency paves way for prominence. A positive attitude helps winners to always see the bright side of anything. They see light while others see only darkness, they see opportunities, while others see only obstacles. To Winners, problems are challenges demanding unused potentials. Where Winners are in control obstacles give Way to miracle.

Such was the attitude of David the man after God's heart. When the armies of Israel saw Goliath too big a problem to handle, he saw Goliath too big an opportunity to miss.

I love the way Glenn Clark illustrated the issue of attitude towards events or problems. Hear him:

> *"One man gets nothing but discord out of a piano; another gets harmony. No one claims the piano is at fault. Life is about the same. The discord is there, and the harmony is there. Study to play it correctly and it will give forth the beauty; play it falsely and it will give forth the ugliness. Life is not at fault."*

TO WINNERS FAILURE IS NEVER FINAL

The easiest thing anybody can do is quit. But no one needs to make quitting a way of life. You can join the winning few by staying put in the right direction with a positive attitude until victory is achieved.

Winners never accept failure as a final result. They see failure as a stage on the track of success but not the end. They keep trying until they succeed. They refuse to die until they are dead.

Albert Einstein failed high school Mathematics. But today his Mathematical theories have brought about dynamic progress in the scientific world. Thomas Edison, the great inventor was asked how it feels to fail seven hundred times trying to invent a practical filament. He said:

> "I have failed not even once, but have proven seven hundred different ways that won't work".

And it was after ten thousand so called failures before Thomas Edison was able to invent a light filament bulb that we now enjoy. He just refused to accept defeat. He never gave up until good result arrived.

Louire Pasture, had a "C" grade in Chemistry in high school. But he developed the pasturisation of milk and a cure for rabbis.

That you've failed before is not what makes you a failure. It is remaining in that position and accepting the circumstance as final.

> "A man is not hurt so much by what happens as by his opinion of what happens"

- Michael De Montaigne

Winners don't just stand and Watch their dreams collapse before their eyes, without doing something about it. They act with a positive attitude before it is too late. They know that everyone has limitations. So they don't keep talking about limitations.

> *"You can never change anything you are willing to tolerate."*
> *- Myles Munroe*

To be a Winner you need not be perfect before being productive. Noah, Abraham, Jacob, David, Solomon and many others all made positive impact. They were imperfect yet, their positive contributions live perfectly forever.

All that is needed is to have a positive attitude towards life. An attitude that believes that with God all things are possible.

REMEMBER

- Your attitude will either make a palace or a prison for you, out of this world.
- Right attitude is the greatest determinant of high performance.
- Everyone can start a marathon race but only the person with a right attitude finishes the race.
- Living in hell or heaven here on earth depends entirely on your attitude to life.

- Nothing reasonable is ever achieved with a negative attitude.

- To overcome the fiery problems of life godliness is required.

- Winners never accept failure as a final result.
- To be a winner you need not be perfect before being productive.

CHAPTER 2

Winners Are Men Qf Integrity
And Good Character

"Integrity is the glue that holds our way of life together. We must constantly strive to keep our integrity intact. When wealth is lost, nothing is lost; when character is lost, all is lost."
- Billy Graham

The integrity of the upright shall guide them: but the perverseness of transgressors shall destroy them.
- Proverbs 11:3

The strongest factor that makes a winner win irrespective of circumstance is his integrity and good character. Integrity ensures consistency; Character ensures stability.
Men of integrity can be read in and out and trusted. A man of good character is dependable.

There is no hidden hypocrisy in him. Integrity is the first step to consistent victory in life. It is the strength of character.

Decide your character and your character will decide your future

In a progressive and godly society, men of integrity are models. Personal integrity advertises a Winner. Good character is the result of determined disciplined life style. You make your own character. No man is born with character.

Character is developed through a steady and consistent behavioral pattern. A man of good character is revealed in crisis. That is why winners are at their best in crisis. What a young man is doing determines to a large extent what he will be in future. The future of a man is a reflection of his character. Decide your character and your character will decide your future.

> *"The measure of a man's character is what he would do If*
> *he would never be found out."*
> *- Thomas Macaulay*

Winners do what they say and say what they do. Their words are their ways, their Words are their bounds, and they never fail to keep a promise. Their lips, hearts, hands and legs play the same rhythm and dance to the same music. Honesty is the best policy of Winners. You can trust them and not be put to shame. They know how to prefer one another in love. Men of good character deserve their victory in life, because a man deserves to be honored more for his character than for his achievements.

Good character procures favor: The favor of man and the favor of God. Such was the reason for the triumph of Joseph in Egypt at the face of the vicissitudes of life. Look at the hurdles Joseph crossed through the strength of his integrity and character.

He was hated and despised for no just cause just like Jesus, his dreams did not conform to the culture and traditions of men.

> *"And his brethren said unto him, Shalt thou indeed reign*
> *over us? Or shalt thou indeed have dominion over us? And*
> *they hated him yet the more for his dreams, and for his*
> *words."*
> *- Genesis 37:8*

For no just cause his brothers envied him. They conspired against him, de-robed him, threw him into the pit and eventually sold him into slavery.

> *"And his brethren envied him; but his father observed the saying …And when they saw him afar off even before he came unto them, they conspired against him to slay him … And it came to pass, when Joseph was come unto his brethren, that they stript Joseph out-of his coat of many colours that was on him. And they took him, and cast him into a pit: and the pit was empty, there was no water in it. And they sat down to eat bread: and they lifted up their eyes and looked, and, behold, a company of Ishmaelites came from Gilead with their camels bearing spicery and balm and myrrh, going to carry it down to Egypt. And Judah said unto his brethren, what profit is it if we slay our brother, and conceal his blood? Come, and let us sell him to the Ishmaelites, and let not our hands be upon him; for he is our brother and our flesh. And his brethren were content. Then there passed by Midianites merchantmen; and they drew and lifted Joseph out of the pit, and sold Joseph to the Ishmaelites for twenty pieces of silver: and they brought Joseph to*
> *Egypt"*
> *- Genesis 37: 11, 18, 23, 24 - 28*

His own brothers desired profit from his misfortune. They cared less about what happened to him as long as the price was right. He knew that the fate of a man is not sealed by crisis. If character is lost, all is lost. So, even when character assassins swooped in on him and he was threatened to compromise his integrity; he preferred the imprisonment of his body than of his soul.

> *"And it came to pass after these things, that his master's wife cast her eyes upon Joseph; and she said, lie with me.*

But he refused, and said unto his master's wife, Behold, my master wotteth not what is with me in the house, and he hath committed all that he hath to my hand;

There is none greater in this house than I; neither hath he kept back anything from me but thee, because thou art his wife: how then can I do this great wickedness, and sin against God?

And it came to pass, as she spake with Joseph day by day, that he harkened not unto her, to lie by her, or to be with her.

And it came to pass about this time that Joseph went into the house to do his business; and there was none of the men of the house there within.

And she caught him by his garment, saying, Lie with me: and he left his garment in her hand, and fled and got him out.

And it came to pass when she saw that he had left his garment in her hand, and was fled forth, That she called unto the men of her house and she spake unto them, saying, See, he hath

brought in an Hebrew unto us to mock us; he came in unto me to lie with me, and I cried with a loud voice:"
- Genesis 39: 7 - 14

"And Joseph's master took him, and put him into the prison, a place where the king's prisoners were bound: and he was there in the prison."
- Genesis 39: 20

Joseph had God's favor to succeed by virtue of his character. God respects character more than charisma. Joseph became prosperous. God blessed him and all that favored him.

"And his master saw that the Lord was with him, and that the Lord made all that he did to prosper in his hand.
And Joseph found grace in his sight, and he served him: and

he made him overseer over his house, and all that he had he
put into his hand.
And it came to pass that from the time that he had made
him overseer in his house, and over all that he had, that the
Lord blessed the Egyptians house for Joseph's sake; and the
blessing of the Lord was upon all that he had in the house;
and in the field. And he left all that he had in Joseph's hand:
and he knew not ought he had, save the bread which he did
eat. And Joseph was a goodly person."
- Genesis 39: 3 - 6

He had the spirit of God and was wise.

"And Pharaoh said unto his servants, can we find such a
one as this is, a man in whom the spirit of God is?
And Pharaoh said unto Joseph, Forasmuch as God hath
shewed thee all this, there is none so discreet and wise as
thou art:"
- Genesis 41:38 – 39

"The wise shall inherit glory: but shame shall be the promo-
tion of fools."
- Proverbs 3: 35

God promoted him to the highest position in the land. In promotion, he was still humble, he was not vengeful He forgave his
brothers that did him evil.

"And Joseph said unto his Brethren, Come near to me, I
pray you. And they came near. And he said I am Joseph
your brother, whom ye sold into Egypt.
Now, therefore do not be grieved, nor angry with your-
selves, that ye sold me hither: for God did send me before
you to preserve life.
...Moreover he kissed all his brethren, and wept upon them:
and after that his brethren talked with him."

- Genesis 45: 4 - 5

When a nation is in crisis only men of integrity can weather the storm successfully. When a man of character is at the top, adequate care for all is top priority. To be at the top you need charisma and character. Charisma may take you to the top, only character can keep you at the top.

REMEMBER

- Integrity is the first step to consistent victory in life.

- Integrity ensures consistency; character ensures stability.

- Good character is the result of a determined disciplined lifestyle.

- Good character procures favor: The favor of man and the favor of God.

- If character is lost, all is lost.

- God respects character more than charisma.

- Charisma may take you to the top, only character can keep you at the top.

CHAPTER 3

Winners Find Something To Offer

"By faith Abel offered unto God a more excellent sacrifice than Cain, by which he obtained witness that he was righteous, God testifying of his gifts: and by it he being dead yet speaketh."
- Hebrew 11 : 4

Winners are those who have found something good to offer God and their generation. If you will ever be counted among the successful, you must find something that satisfies market demands, friends and relatives. Not just anything, It must be something excellent that will outlive you.

Abel was counted among Winners of his generation because he offered a more excellent gift. By this offering, he obtained a witness that he was righteous. Even after death his gift still speaks. Excellent impacts hardly expire.

The secret of outstanding promotion lies in having something to offer

Jephthah in Judges ll was thrown out of his father's house, out of his inheritance. His brothers called him the son of a harlot. They felt he had nothing to offer. He became an orphan.

If you have nothing to offer, you become an orphan. Nobody will be ready to 'father' you. You will have no mother. Have a close look at those being called "my son", "my daughter" by people who are not their biological parents. You will find that it is because they have something to offer their "fathers" and their "mothers".

After Jephthah was thrown out, he went to look for something others lacked, to offer. He trained himself in warfare. He soon became very strong and was now an irresistible and marketable commodity. His market value had been improved. And the once rejected orphan was now in demand. When the enemies of his Hebrew family threatened to wipe them out, Jephthah was called to their defense with an offer of the much desired throne, to rule and reign over his brethren.

You can't rule and reign in this world with nothing to offer. Even God, our Almighty Father and creator cherishes an excellent offering.

> *"And Solomon went up thither to the brazen altar before the Lord, which was at the tabernacle of the congregation, and offered a thousand burnt offerings upon it. In that night did God appear unto Solomon, and said unto him, ask what I shall give thee."*
> *-2 Chronicles 1 : 6 – 7*

Solomon offered God a thousand offerings and went to sleep asking nothing from God. God had to wake him up that night in order to bless him. Many have been asking and praying for so long and have nothing to show for it. Try this out. Find something excellent to offer God. Do something for God and wait to see God offer you your heart's desires. Big offerings bring big blessings.

> *"And Noah builded an altar unto the Lord; and took of every clean beast, and of every clean fowl, and offered burnt offerings on the altar.*

> *And the Lord smelled a sweet savour; and the LORD said*
> *in his heart, I will not again curse the ground anymore for*
> *man's sake; For the imagination of man's heart is evil from*
> *his youth; neither will I again smite anymore everything*
> *living, as l have done.*
> *While the earth remaineth, seedtime and harvest, and cold*
> *and heat, and summer and winter, and day and night shall*
> *not cease."*
> *- Genesis 8:20-22*

Noah offered God a sweet smelling sacrifice. This caused God not only to decree never to curse the ground again, but also to establish the law of seedtime and harvest time.

Joseph would have died a prisoner if he had nothing to offer Pharaoh. He offered Pharaoh the interpretation of his dream, and Pharaoh offered him rulership and authority.

> *"And Pharaoh said unto Joseph, Forasmuch as God has*
> *shown thee all this, there is none so discreet and wise as*
> *thou art; Thou shalt be over my house, and according unto*
> *thy word shall all my people be ruled: only in the throne will*
> *I be greater than thou. And Pharaoh said unto Joseph, See,*
> *I have set thee over all the land of Egypt."*
> *-Genesis 41: 39 – 41*

You can't ascend the throne unless you have something to offer. Joseph. Was not the only one in prison at that time. There were many other people in there with him. They probably never regained their freedom. What you have to offer can purchase for you liberty and freedom from poverty and financial humiliation.

Abraham's commitment and offering of Isaac to God made him a father of many nations. He became a friend of God. No person will befriend you if you have nothing to offer. The offering of his only son to God also procured for us God's offering of his only begotten Son that brought us salvation.

Cornelius offered alms to the poor and prayers to God in his time. By these, he built a monument: a memorial before God. And although we read that God does not hear sinners, this sinners' voice was heard in the high heavens by reason of what he offered.

> *"There was a certain man in Caesarea called Cornelius, a centurion of the band called the Italian band, A devout man, and one that feared God with all his house, which gave much alms to the people, and prayed to God always.*
> *He saw in a vision evidently about the ninth hour of the day an angel of God coming in to him, and saying unto him, Cornelius. And when he looked on him, he was afraid, and asked, What is it, Lord? And he said unto him, Thy prayers and thine alms are come up for a memorial before God."*
> *-Acts 10 : 1- 4*

God had to compel Peter the undisputed leader of the apostles to personally present the message and gift of salvation to Cornelius.

You Want salvation from poverty, sicknesses and diseases, offer God your life, your heart, your time and you will become a winner.

You Can Offer Service

Joshua the son of Nun offered Moses excellent service and Moses in turn treated him like a son. Through impartation form Moses he received the spirit of wisdom and favor above his fellows.

> *"And Joshua the son of Nun was full of the spirit of wisdom; for Moses had laid his hands upon him: and the children of Israel harkened unto him, and did as the Lord commanded*

Moses."
- Deuteronomy 34 : 9

Elisha served his master Elijah and his country Israel diligently to the end. Elijah offered him a double portion of the anointing. The secret of outstanding promotion lies in having something to offer.

> *"And it came to pass, when they had gone over, that Elijah said unto Elisha, Ask what I shall do for thee, before I be taken away from thee. And Elisha said, I pray thee, let a double portion of thy spirit be upon me.*
> *And he said, Thou hast asked a hard thing: nevertheless, if thou see me when I am taken from thee, it shall be so unto thee; but if not it shall not be so. And it came to pass, as they still went on, and talked, that, behold, there appeared a chariot of fire, and horses of fire and parted them both asunder; and Elijah went up by the whirlwind into heaven. And Elisha saw it, and he cried, My father, My father, the chariots of Israel, and the horsemen thereof And he saw him no more: and he took hold his own clothes, and rent them in two pieces.*
> *He took up also the mantle of Elijah that fell from him, and went back, and stood by the bank of Jordan;*
> *And He took the mantle of Elijah that fell from him, and smote the waters, and said, Where is the Lord God of Elijah? And when he also had smitten the waters, they parted hither and thither: and Elisha went over.*
> *And when the sons of the prophets who were to view at Jericho saw him, they said, the spirit of Elijah doth rest on Elisha. And they came to meet him, and bowed themselves to the ground before him."*
> *- 2 Kings 2: 9 - 15*

Everyman has something to offer. Find yours. Something at which you are at your best. Develop yourself in that area. You may have been a looser: you can become a Winner by developing your gifts and talents to offer the World something good. Winners are ex-loosers who found something to offer. Your offering can give you a place in the hall of winners.

REMEMBER

- Winners are those who have found something to offer God and their generation.

- Excellent Impacts hardly expire.

- If you have nothing to offer, you become an orphan.

- You can't rule and reign in this world with nothing to offer.

- Big offerings bring big blessings.

- What you have to offer can purchase for you liberty and freedom from poverty and financial humiliation.

- No person will befriend you if you have nothing to offer.

- Winners are ex-loosers who found something to offer.

CHAPTER 4

Winners Look Inward To Go Forward

"Ye are of God, little children, and have overcome them; because greater is he that is in you, than he that is in the world."
-l John 4:4

God has potentials deposited in every man: assets of talents, gifts and special endowments. Winners are people who found an asset within them and developed the assets for profitable results.

The inventors, great singers, renowned sport men and women, successful industrialists, financial heavyweights, and outstanding political leaders are all in this group. They undergo spiritual, marital and physical discipline in order to fully harness the inner strength given them by God. There is no one without special ability.

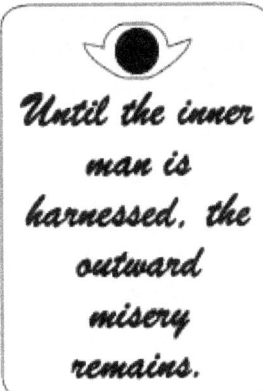

Until the inner man is harnessed, the outward misery remains.

Those who will succeed in life are those who will maximize every God given ability and resource at their disposal, thereby, achieving their goal in life. So, look inward to go upward.

God has put in and around you facilitators of success. And you can never be a winner without using them. The life of Moses as seen in the book of Exodus indicates this.

> *"And he said unto him, what is in thy hand? And he said,*
> *A rod. And he said, cast it on the ground. And he cast it on*
> *the ground, and it became a serpent: and Moses fled from*
> *before it. And the Lord said unto Moses, put forth thy hand,*
> *and take it by the tail. And he put forth his hand, and*
> *caught it, and it became a rod in his hand: That they may*
> *believe that the Lord God of their fathers, the God of Abra-*
> *ham, God of Isaac, God of Jacob, hath appeared unto thee."*
> *- Exodus 4: 2 – 5*

This rod had been with Moses all along. It was given to him for signs and wonders that would bring deliverance to his people from the hands of the Egyptians. It had to be cast down for it to act. If your potential is not cast down, it can never gain kinetic energy. Moses did not value the rod until God called his attention to it.

May I call your attention to your rod this day? It is right there with you. Every man of depth has made a personal discovery. Did you notice that it was called the rod of God later? Value your God given talents.

> *"So Moses took his wife and sons and put them on a donkey,*
> *and returned to the land of Egypt, holding tightly to the*
> *'rod of God."*
> *- Exodus 4: 20*

The bible says he held on tightly to the rod. It was by this rod that God made Moses a god unto Pharaoh.

> *"And the Lord said unto Moses, See I have made thee a god*
> *to Pharaoh: and Aaron thy brother shall be thy prophet."*
> *- Exodus 7:1*

At the Red Sea when faith was about failing his people, God called his attention to the rod.

> *"And the Lord said unto Moses, Wherefore criest thou unto me? Speak unto the children of Israel, that they go forward: But lift up thy rod, and stretch out thine hand over the sea, and divide it: and the children of Israel shall go on dry ground through the midst of the sea."*
> *- Exodus 14: 15 – 16*

If you will ever make meaningful progress, make deliberate effort to look inward for your rod. Harness your inner assets before looking about for other people's assets to use. Lift up your rod to lift up your life.

The case of Gideon was not different. God had deposited in him awesome power for the liberation of his people from the hands of the Midianites. He was hiding and looking for the external intervention of God.

> *"And the angel of the Lord appeared unto him, and said unto him, The lord is with thee, thou mighty man of valour. And Gideon said unto him, Oh my lord, If the Lord be with us, why then is all these befallen us? And where be all his miracles, which our fathers told us of, saying, did not the Lord bring us up from Egypt? But now has forsaken us, and delivered us into the hands of the Midianites.*
> *And the Lord looked upon him, and said, Go in this thy might, and thou shall save Israel from the hands of the Midianites: have not I sent thee?*
> *And he said unto him, Oh Lord, wherewith shall I save Israel? Behold, my family is poor in Manasseh, and I am the least in my father's house."*
> *-Judges 6 : 12 - 15*

God's command to him was "Go in this thy might". Instead of

lamenting your poverty and the poverty surrounding you, do something with the "might" inside of you. Greater is he that is in you than the poverty that is in the world. Until the inner man is harnessed, the outward misery remains. Enough of lamentation! Lamentation has never delivered anyone from lameness. Only the inward strength can give you the outward movement. Posterity will not forgive you if you carry the resources of God within you into the grave without using them for the benefit of humanity.

> *"... For unto whomsoever much is given, of him shall be much required: and to whom men have committed much, of him they will ask the more."*
> *- Luke 12:48*

REMEMBER

- Winners are people who have found assets within them and developed the assets for profitable results.

- Those who will succeed in life are those who will maximize their God given ability to achieve their goal in life.

- Posterity will never forgive you if you carry the resources of God into the grave.

- Only the inward strength can give you the outward movement.

- Greater is he that is in you than the poverty that is in the world.

CHAPTER 5

Winners Are Well Informed

The difference between success and failure could just be information or lack of it. In God's formulae of success, information is an indispensable factor.

Information brings about transformation in life and business. Little Wonder there is so much investment in Information Technology. A lack of information produces deformation. The extent of divine transformation experienced depends largely on the amount of divine information at one's disposal.

Information is a powerful weapon: it is a fighting force. The developed nations are what they are today because of the amount of information at their disposal.

Information edge gives swift victory

> "Wisdom hath built her house, she hath hewn out her seven pillars."
> - Proverbs 9: 1

Countries send out spies to other countries to have an information edge. This is because an information edge gives swift victory in any competitive market, struggle or war among nations.

Whoever has accurate information about the strength and weakness of his opponent brightens his chances of winning the battle.

"A wise man is strong; yea, a man of knowledge increaseth strength. For by wise counsel thou shall make thy war; and in multitude of counsellors there is safety."
- Proverbs 24: 5 - 6

"A wise man is mightier than a strong man. Wisdom is mightier than strength. Don't go to war without wise guidance; there is safety in many counsellors."
- Proverbs 24 : 5 - 6 (TLB)

The Wars of the 21st Century are going to be fought and won only by the amount of divine information and technological knowledge we have. The devil and calamities are close to those who live in ignorance. Visions and ideas are destroyed by lack of information.

"My people are destroyed for lack of knowledge: because thou has rejected knowledge, I will also reject thee, that thou shall be no priest to me; seeing that thou hast forgotten the law of thy God, I will also forget thy children."
- Hosea 4 : 6

Jesus fought the devil and shook him away because he had an information edge. Christ's fighting weapon was divine information.

"But he answered and said; it is written, man shall not live by bread alone, but by every word that proceedeth out of the mouth of God."
- Matthew 4:4

WINNERS RULE BY WISDOM

Accurate information will elevate you and re-position you to achieve great heights.

"The fear of the Lord is the beginning of wisdom: and the knowledge of the Holy is understanding."
- Proverbs 9: 10

Information gives knowledge and knowledge brings understanding. No meaningful victory is achieved without knowledge. A good knowledge of God will help any man to do exploits in every realm of life.

"...But the people that do know their God shall be strong, and do exploits."
- Daniel 11:32

Wisdom is needed to sail through the stormy waters of life. And Wisdom is the correct application of knowledge with the understanding gained through the information at our disposal.

The fear of God puts you on wisdom lane.

"Get wisdom, get understanding: forget it not; neither decline from the words of my mouth. Forsake her not, and she shall preserve thee: love her, and she shall keep thee."
-Proverbs 4: 5 – 6

"Then said I Wisdom is better than strength . . ."
- Ecclesiastes 9:16a

"Wisdom is better than weapons of war... "
- Ecclesiastes 9: 18a

Winners who rule the world, rule and reign by wisdom. Dominion is impossible without wisdom.

"By me kings reign, and princes decree justice. By me princes rule, and nobles, even all the judges of the earth."

- Proverbs 8: 15 – 16

REMEMBER

- In God's formula for success, information is an indispensable factor.
- The extent of divine transformation experienced depends on the amount of divine information at one's disposal.
- Information is a fighting force.
- Visions and ideas are destroyed by lack of information.
- The fear of God puts you on wisdom lane.

- Dominion is impossible without wisdom.

CHAPTER 6

Winners Are Great Thinkers

"For as he thinketh in his heart, so he..."
- Proverbs 23 : 7

"Whatever the mind of man can conceive and believe it will achieve."
- Napoleon Hill

Our mental attitude determines a lot of things. The way you act in every situation stems from the way you think. Your personality has a strong relationship with your thought. What you think is what you take. Insightful godly thoughts can produce the power to change the course of destiny.

If your heart cannot conceive it in thought, your hands will not achieve it.

Winners are men of sound mind. They think their way to the top. They think success, victory, prosperity, and righteousness all the days of their lives.

Your thinking defines where you are heading. You need to think success for you to act for success. If your heart cannot conceive it in thought, your hands will refuse to go into action to achieve it. Thoughts are a creative force. The way you think in your heart will create what you say. And what you say is what you have.

"For verily I say unto you, that whosoever shall say unto this mountain, be thou removed, and be thou cast into the sea; And shall not doubt in his heart, but shall believe that those things which he sayeth shall come to pass; he shall have whatsoever he sayeth. Therefore I say unto you, what things so ever ye desire when ye pray believe that ye receive them and ye shall have them."
- Mark 11:23-24

Winners Think Their Way Out Of Sin And Poverty

"Health is the product of man's capacity to think."
- Ayn Ranal

"Come now, and let us reason together sayeth the Lord."
- Isaiah 1:18

You can reason with God out of poverty. You can reason your way out of failure. You can reason with God out of Sin. He says come now, right now, let us reason together let us rub our minds and weigh issues as they ought to be so that you can live a worthwhile life. Winners tread on this path.

Winners know that he who refuses to reason with God has no reason for living and will never be a reasonable person.

"And when he finally came to his senses, he said to himself...."
- Luke 15:17 (TLB)

When the prodigal son became reasonable, he was on his way out of suffering. He did not say any prayer to get out of poverty and sin. He thought his way out of problems. His thinking led him to repentance. He came to himself; he sat down to think.

Winners take time out to sit down. You need to stop this running around and making no progress. Think — what have I been doing wrong? What have I been doing right? What should I do right to make progress? Sit down and ponder to prosper.

"For who hath known the mind Of the Lord, that he may instruct him? But we have the mind of Christ."
- 1 Corinthians 2:16

God is Mindful of What You Think

"...He is able to do exceedingly above all that we ask or think."
- Ephesians 3:20

God can do not only what you ask but what you think. Notice the bible says *".... All that we ask or think."* God can do what we think. If we think victory, He will give victory. If you think failure, you will have failure. Champions of all shades are aware of this spiritual fact.

So, renew your mind daily with God's news if you need good news.

YOU POSSES THE MIND OF GOD

"For God has not given us the spirit of fear but of power, of love and of a sound mind."
- 2 Timothy 1:7

If you are born again and filled with the Holy Ghost, You possess a sound mind. You have the creative mind of God.

"For who hath known the mind of the Lord, that he may

instruct him? But we have the mind of Christ."
- I Corinthians 2:16

Great inventions and scientific achievements came about through the power of thoughts. Creation takes place in the mind before being translated into reality. Thought is the breeding ground of all riches. And God has given man the power to take control of his thoughts. That is why accurate thinking is one valuable asset that must be meticulously groomed.

A man who can take full possession of his own mind can take full possession of anything. The thoughts you think and the things you do now will determine your tomorrow. Your destination is fashioned out in your thoughts and actions.

To remain Godly you must think godly thoughts. To prosper, think prosperity thoughts. To win, think winning thoughts. To be healthy, think healthy thoughts.

> *"It is not enough to have a good mind: the main thing is to use it well."*
> *-Rene Descartes*

YOU CAN ARREST EVIL REASONING

> *"Casting down imaginations, and every high thing that exalteth itself against the knowledge of God, and bringing into captivity every thought to the obedience of Christ."*
> *- 2 Corinthians 10:5*

You can overcome improper thinking. The original word 'Imagination' can be translated 'reasoning'. So, cast down any reasoning that rises above what the bible says about you. Bring into captivity every thought, every reasoning to the obedience of Christ. Your reasoning must be in agreement with God's word for it to produce the needed result.

Change your negative thoughts and your future will change.

WHAT TO THINK ON

"Whatsoever things are true
Whatsoever things are honest
Whatsoever things are just
Whatsoever things are pure
Whatsoever things are lovely
Whatsoever things are of good report
If there be any virtue
And if there be any praise,
Think on these things."
- Philippians 4:8

With this kind of thinking you are unstoppable. Right thinking is a product of divine revelation. And the quality of your thinking goes a long Way to determine the quality of your life.

FACT THINKING VERSUS FAITH THINKING

Fact knowledge produces fact thinking. Faith knowledge produces faith thinking. Faith thinking is superior and divine. Fact knowledge comes from the visible world and the things in the visible world are temporal and subject to change. Thoughts and actions based on physical facts can be faulty. Faith knowledge comes from God's declaration. Thinking based on these, produces eternal results.

REMEMBER

- Your personality has a strong relationship with your thought.
- Insightful godly thoughts can produce the power to change the course of destiny.
- He who refuses to reason with God has no reason for living and will never be a reasonable person.
- Renew your mind daily with God's news you need good news.
- Right thinking is a product of divine revelation.
- Thought is the breeding ground of all riches.
- Your thoughts and actions fashion out your destiny.
- Faith knowledge produces faith thinking and this gives eternal results.

CHAPTER 7

Winners Are Good Time Managers

Time is the most valuable resource available to mankind. Nothing else compares to it, yet it is the most wasted resource. Time can be expended but it cannot be replenished. The most painful regrets of the latter years of life come from wasted years. Time waits for no man. It moves forward but never backwards.

All successful men have developed the habit of employing the time resource profitably. They know that the difference between success and failure lies in how well and for what purpose a man uses his time. Time can be spent, wasted or killed. But be warned killing time is suicidal.

Time is the most valuable resource available to man.

What a man becomes in his future depends largely on what he does with his time in the present. If you sit down and do nothing with your time, you become a no — thing in time. This is because time will be used up whether you employ it or not.

> *"To every thing there is a season, and a time to every purpose under heaven."*
> *- Ecclesiastes 3:1*

> *"To every thing there is a season, and a time for every mat-*

ter or purpose under heaven:"
- Ecclesiastes 3:1 (Amplified)

"We have time enough if we will use it right."
- Johann Wolfgans Von Goethe

There is adequate time for every good purpose. Those who blame their failure on lack of time are insincere. Everyone has twenty-four hours a day, seven days a week, and three hundred and sixty five days in a normal year. Failure does not arise from inadequate time but from inadequate use at time for meaningful purpose.

"Jesus answered, Are there not twelve hours in the day? If any man walk in the day, he stumbleth not, because he seeth the light of this world. But if a man walk in the night, he stumbleth, because there is no light in him.
These things said he: and after that he said unto them, Our friend Lazarus sleepeth; but I go, that I may wake him out of his sleep."
- John 11:9-11

There are also appointed times and seasons of change for any purpose under the sun. Discernment of God's time and season is necessary in order to co-operate with God in purposeful action that brings victory.

"I said in mine heart, God shall judge the righteous and the wicked: for there is a time there for every purpose and for every work."
- Ecclesiastes 3:17

"Thou shall arise and have mercy upon Zion: for the time to favor her, yea, the set time, is come."
- Psalms 102:13

God has a set time to favor his own. It is dangerous to walk out on Him and do nothing when the set time of God to favor us has come. Remaining as part of God's family signs you on for divine favor.

> *"He hath made everything beautiful in his time: also He hath set the world in their heart, so that no man can find out the work that God maketh from the beginning to the end."*
> *- Ecclesiastes 3:11*

The above scriptures show that the beauty of a thing is directly related to the time. This means that a good thing can be ugly if done at the wrong time. The news of a pregnant eleven-year-old student is ugly while the news of a pregnant matured married woman is beautiful.

Winners have a good understanding of time. They are good time managers who know how to do the right thing at the right time. They are not easily overtaken by events. They are proactive and not reactive. The children of Issachar were men of such understanding.

> *"And of the children of Issachar, which were men that had an understanding of the times, to know what Israel ought to do; the heads of them were two hundred; and all their brethren were at their commandment."*
> *- 1 Chronicles 12:32*

The mastering of time involves arranging our work each day in such a way as to enable us do things that are important rather than those things that are urgent. Important things are those with long term positive impact while urgent ones are those screaming for attention. Stress does result from misuse of time and inability to meet with deadlines.

Many people say time is money. That is not true, time is much more than money. Much money can be gained in a short time, but time cannot be regained. An hour lost is lost forever. Time mastering is a skill winners strive to acquire.

> "A fool may waste money, but the greatest fool wastes time."

Give the most of your time to the most important issues of life. Winners focus on the successful completion of any project they undertake. This focus and determination will control your experience of time management.

> "Time flies. It is up to you to be the pilot."
> - J.L. Mason

REMEMBER

- Time can be expended but it cannot be replaced.

- The most painful regrets of later years of life come from wasted years

- Killing time is suicidal.

- If you sit down and do nothing with your time, you become no-thing in time.

- Failure arise from inadequate use of time for meaningful purpose.

- The beauty of a thing is related to its time.

- Time mastery is a skill winners strive to acquire.

- Give the most of your time to the most important issues of life.

CHAPTER 8

Winners Overcome Fear By Faith

Fear is success' enemy number one. Winners are those who have learnt to shut the door against fear using the key of faith in God. It is obvious to Winners that the devil is the source of evil. Whenever he wants to launch his operation S.K.D.- (stealing, killing and destroying), he uses the gateway of fear.

Some loosers are born in fear; they live in fear and die in fear. Anyone who lives in fear and relishes in worrying is in danger of failing always. Fear prepares the ground for failure. It is the entry visa for failure to take hold. Job feared that he might loose all that God had given him and it came to pass.

Where faith is in place, fear will never take root.

> *"For the thing which I greatly feared is come upon me, and that which I was afraid of is come unto me."*
> *-Job 3:25*

Fear allows the hedge of protection to be broken. Fear brings reproach. Fear drives away friends. Whoever is ruled by fear, is first in the kingdom of failures. Fear hinders accomplishment. Fear demobilizes and demoralizes, it discourages actions, and it turns giants into Lilliputians. It is a powerful wear and tear agent. Fear has torment.

"There is no fear in love; but perfect love casteth out fear:
because fear hath torment.
He that feareth is not made perfect in love."
- 1 John 4:18

Fear breeds sickness: it reduces the life span of the host. It has a gradual killing effect on the host. Nothing else drains strength more than fear. Nothing punishes like fear. Faith furnishes the host, but fear punishes the host. Fear breeds cowardice and timidity.

Winners always conquer this monster mother of cowards through the action of faith. The victory comes over fear when we believe God's facts as presented by the scriptures. Having faith in God and in yourself coupled with necessary action will help to cure fear.

FEAR IS A SPIRIT

"For God has not given us the spirit of fear; but of power,
and of love, and of a sound mind."
- 2 Timothy 1:7

Fear is a spirit, not just an emotional thing. This spirit that brings destruction, comes from the devil. It is a very possessive spirit. Fear makes you see evil even when the is none. It gives you the feeling of the possibility of evil and danger.

No wonder someone defined fear as False Evidence Appearing Real. Wherever evil report is believed, fear thrives. Fear is a dominating spirit, it freezes action. But faith propels action.

"For whatsoever is born of God overcometh the world: and
this is the victory that overcometh the world, even our
faith."
- 1 John 5:4

FAITH PUTS GOD IN ACTION

Someone defined faith as:
Forsaking
All
I
Trust
Him

Faith crushes every opposition and makes every desire obtainable. Where there is no faith there can be no breakthrough. Where faith is in place fear will never take root. Winners live by faith.

> *"Now the just shall live by faith: but if any man draw back, my soul shall have no pleasure in him."*
> *- Hebrews 10:38*

Faith is the way to be first. Faith never denies reality. But it is the acknowledgement of the supremacy of God's point of view.

Faith puts God in action. Fear puts the devil in action. There are seven deadly fears that Winners detest.

§ **The Fear Of Man:** The fear of man is What makes sinners deny God. It enslaves and makes men tell lies.

> *"The fear of man bringeth a snare: but whoso putteth his trust in the Lord shall be safe."*
> *- Proverbs 29:25*

> *"Let your conversation be without covetousness; and be content with such things as ye have: for he hath said: I will never leave thee, nor forsake thee.*
> *So that we may boldly say, The Lord is my helper, and I will not fear what man shall do unto me."*
> *- Hebrews 13:5-6*

§ **The Fear Of Rejection:** This evil spirit makes you feel inadequate, unfit and withdrawn. Those bound by this fear are lone-rangers. They are dangerous to the society. Winners overcome this by the realization of their peculiarity. When you know that you are special, fearfully and wonderfully made you will learn to accept who you are. God never makes misfits.

§ **The Fear Of Failure:** Men who are bound by this evil are always afraid to take risks. But no man rises without risks. The person not taking risks is risking failure. Winners overcome this fear by being courageous in all their undertakings. They are -aware that the courage to take risks is the key to success.

> *"Nay, in all these things we are more than conquerors through him that loved us."*
> *- Romans 8:37*

> *"I can do all things through Christ which strengthens me."*
> *- Philippians 4:13*

> *"Now thanks be unto God, which always causeth us to triumph in Christ, and maketh manifest the savor of his knowledge by us in every place."*
> *- 2 Corinthians 2:14*

§ **Fear Of The Future:** This spirit makes one worry about what the future holds. Worrying is like a rocking chair. It makes movement. The movement makes you go round and round on the same spot with no achievement. Worrying gets nothing done. It is a time waster, it is unproductive. Worrying magnifies uncertainties. This fear encourages superstition, and makes men consult all kinds of fortunetellers. Winners rely on the promises of God for their future. They are never afraid of the future. For they know that:

> "... all things work together for good to them that love God,
> to them who are the called according to his purpose."
> - Romans 8:28

§ **Fear Of Poverty:** This fear encourages greed. It makes man hoard goods. And hoarding produces more scarcity. Many in this world are held hostage by the fear of poverty. This spirit stops men from giving. It makes nations to enter into war with other nations. The damaging effect of this spirit is what we now have in the increase in armed robberies, killing and stealing all over the earth. Winners understand God to be a God of abundance who takes pleasure in the prosperity of his own.

> "He that spared not his own Son, but delivered him up for us all, how shall he not with him also freely give us all things?"
> - Romans 8:32

> "According as his divine power hath given unto us all things that pertain unto life and Godliness, through the knowledge of him that hath called us to glory and virtue: "
> - 2 Peter 1:3

> "But my God shall supply all your need according to his riches in glory by Christ Jesus."
> - Philippians 4:19

§ **The Fear Of ILL Health**: Evil reports from medical personnel usually supply this fear from the devil. This kind of fear makes men die many times before their death. It makes men suspect typhoid fever when symptoms of ordinary fever manifest. Any one bound by this spirit becomes too selective of what they eat and what they drink. They feel pursued by cancer, aids and what have you.

Hear what makes winners immune against these attacks:

> *"That it might be fulfilled which was spoken by Esaias the prophet, saying, Himself took our infirmities, and bare our sicknesses."*
> *- Matthew 8:17*

> *"Surely he hath borne our griefs, and carried our sorrows: yet we did esteem him stricken, smitten of God, and afflicted.*
> *But he was wounded for our transgressions, he was bruised for our iniquities: the chastisement of our peace was upon him; and with his stripes we were healed."*
> *- Isaiah 53:4-5*

§ The Fear Of Death: The pangs and grips of the fear of death are the strongest when compared to all others. Men literally give up when faced with this fear. Everyone has an appointment with death. Winners no longer have the fear of death. Christ has delivered us from the sting and power of death. Through his death and resurrection the believer now has power over the spirit of death.

> *"O death, where is thy sting? O grave, where is thy victory?*
> *The sting of death is sin; the strength of sin is the law.*
> *But thanks be to God, which giveth us the victory through our Lord Jesus Christ."*
> *- I Corinthians 15:55-57*

Hear David who foresaw what winners now enjoy.

> *"Even when walking through the dark valley of death I will*

> *not be afraid, for you are close beside me, guarding, guid-*
> *ing all the way."*
> *- Psalms 23:4(TLB)*

David did not allow the fear of the size of Goliath to weaken him. He overcame Goliath by faith.

Fear is an enemy and God has given us enough arsenals to fight it. In the Holy Bible alone, there are more than 365 'fear nots.' So take a daily dose of God's prescription and fear will banish from your life.

REMEMBER

- Fear is success enemy number one.

- Fear is the entry visa for failure to take hold.

- Whoever is ruled by fear is first in the kingdom of failures.

- Fear is a powerful wear and tear agent.

- Fear punishes the host but faith furnishes the host.

- Fear freezes action but faith propels action.

- Faith is the way to be first.

- The courage to take risks is the key to success.
- Fear makes men die many times before their death.
- Take a daily dose of God's prescription for fear and fear will banish from your life.

CHAPTER 9

Winners Are Courageous

"And Moses called unto Joshua, and said unto him in the sight of all Israel, Be strong and of a good courage: for thou must go with this people unto the land which the Lord hath sworn unto their fathers to give them; and thou shalt cause them to inherit it."
- Deuteronomy 31:7

Winners have courage to stand for what is right. When all around them turn their backs, Winners are not afraid to stand alone. They are aware that God is on the right side. They still keep to what is good even when evil is pleasurable. They endure when it hurts. They are not afraid to tell the truth when a lie is most acceptable. They have courage to pursue their goals when it is no more interesting.

Courage is said to be fear that has said its prayers.

Courage is defined as bravery; the ability to control fear in the face of adversity, danger, pain and hardship. It is being able to say or do what is right under any circumstance. Courage is doing what you are naturally afraid to do. Courage is said to be the fear that has said its prayer. Winners manifest this daring trait.

"Be strong and courageous, be not afraid nor dismayed for the king of Assyria, nor for all the multitude that is with

him: for there be more with us than with him.
With him is the arm of flesh: but with us is the Lord our God
to help us, and to fight our battles. And the peoples rested
themselves on the words of Hezekiah king of Judah."
- 2 Chronicles 32:7-8

One man with courage is greater than a majority that lacks courage. There can be no courage where men are not naturally scared. Courage is acting on a need greater than self. The progress in any life expands in proportion to the courage with which issues are handled.

Winners seek the help of God and face the future with courage. No battle scares the courageous man. He is up when others are down. When men are cast down he is able to say there is a lifting up.

"And David said to Saul, Let no man's heart fail because of
him; thy servant will go and fight with this Philistine."
- 1 Samuel 17:32

More than anything else, It was courage that gave David victory over Goliath. It takes courage to conquer. All true champions are men of courage. What all the men of war of Israel could not face, one man with courage conquered.

Whenever giants in whatever forms rise up to obstruct, winners resort to courage. If courage is not in place, ultimate victory is elusive. God had to emphasize this time and time again to Joshua, when Israel was closing in on the Promised Land.

"Be strong and of a good courage: for unto this people thou
shall divide for an inheritance the land, which I sware unto
their fathers to give them.
Only be thou strong and very courageous, that thou mayest
observe to do according to all the law, which Moses my ser-
vant commanded thee: turn not from it to the right hand

or to the left, that thou mayest prosper witherso-ever thou goest."
-Joshua 1:6-7

Who ever desires to triumph in life needs courage to face reality. Courage to pursue substance rather than shadows that appeal to the emotions of men. Courage to go for what will last. Courage to say no to sin, to say no to evil that enslaves.

Winners take courage to make decisions. They are not men that hang on for long in between two opinions.

> *"And Elijah came unto all the people, and said, How long halt ye between two opinions? If the Lord be God, follow him: but if Baal, follow him. And the people answered him not a word."*
> *- 1 Kings 18:21*

Whether their decision is popular or not, they make bold to take the right step. That is what makes them win all the time when others are loosing. People with courage to make decisions always prevail.

> *"And if it seem evil unto you to serve the Lord, choose ye this day whom you will serve; whether the gods which your fathers served that were on the other side of the flood, or the gods of the Amorites, in whose land ye dwell: but as for me and my house, we will serve the Lord."*
> *-Joshua 24:15*

Caleb and Joshua were also men of good courage. When the multitude of the children of Israel that went to spy the land brought evil report, they stood courageously out of the crowd to give a good report.

> *"And Caleb stilled the people before Moses, and said, Let us*

go up at once, and possess it; for we are well able to over-
come it.'"
- Numbers 13:30

"And Joshua the son of Nun, and Caleb the son of Je-
phunneh, which were of them that searched the land, rent
their clothes:
And they spake unto all the company of the children of Is-
rael, saying, The land, which we passed through to search
it, is an exceeding good land. If the Lord delight in us, then
he will bring us into this land, and give it us; a land which
floweth with milk and honey.
Only rebel ye not against the Lord neither fear ye the people
of the land; for they are bread for us; their defence is de-
parted from them, and the Lord is with us: fear them not."
- Numbers 14:6-9

Indecision breeds indiscipline. God hates indecision. With God
you are either on His side or against Him. Where there is no courage, fear takes over.

Winners use courage to change. Whether the change means personal loss or not, as long as the will of God is done, they are happy.
Whenever God demands repentance, they embrace a turn around.

"And when Asa heard these words, and the prophecy of
Oded the prophet, he took courage, and put away the
abominable idols out of all the land of Judah and Benja-
min, and out of the cities...
... And all Judah rejoiced at the oath; for they had sworn
with all their heart, and sought him with their whole de-
sire; and he was found of them, and the Lord gave them rest
round about."
- 2 Chronicles 15: 8, 15

King Asa was such a man of courage. When idolatry became the order of the day; when immorality became pervasive and operative in the land, he took courage to change after hearing the message of God. No Wonder the bible says there was no more war for a long time. God respects the courage of champions.

> *"And there was no more war unto the five and thirtieth year of the reign of Asa. "*
> *- 2 Chronicles 15:19*

Winners have a desire to prosper. As a result, they have the courage to admit wrong.

> *"He that covereth his sins shall not prosper: but whoso confesseth and forsaketh them shall have mercy."*
> *- Proverbs 28:13*

They don't believe in cover — up. David was such a man. He always had the courage to admit wrong. No Wonder he was called a man after God's own heart. Little wonder also that he never lost any battle. Winners admit when they are wrong.

> *"For I acknowledge my transgressions: and my sin is ever before me. Against thee; thee alone have I sinned and done this evil in thy sight: that thou mightest be justified when thou speakest, and be clear when thou judgest."*
> *- Psalm 51:3 – 4*

Winners take courage to hold on to their convictions. Because Winners are men of strong beliefs, they are men of faith. The winds of persecutions may blow, but the courageous spirits of winners enables them to stand firm on their convictions.

> *"And they called them, and commanded them not to speak at all nor teach in the name of*
> *Jesus. But Peter and John said unto them, whether it be right in the sight of God to hearken unto you more than*

unto God, judge ye.
For we cannot but speak the things which we have seen and
heard."
- Acts 4: 18 – 20

The early apostles were able to turn the world upside down; the right side up because they were not ready to compromise their convictions. No man can have serious impact in this fast moving generation without strong convictions. And it takes courage to have strong convictions. Shadrach, Meshach and Abednego defied the fiery furnace of Babylon courtesy of the courage of their convictions.

Daniel went to the lion's den and came out alive because he had the courage to hold on to his convictions.

If courage can have this soothing effect over fires and lions, your winning on this earth depends on it.

WHAT GIVES GOOD COURAGE

The reality of the presence of God is the greatest source of good courage. No wonder Paul declared boldly:

> *"What shall we then say to these things? If God be for us*
> *who can be against as?"*
> *- Romans 8: 31*

The presence of God instills confidence. When you come to the realization that greater is he that is in you than he that is in the world, no problem is too difficult to overcome. The greater one brings greater rewards.

The word of God is a vital source of good courage. Peter the Apostle demonstrated this when he dared to act on the word of Jesus Christ inspite of the fact that it sounded unreasonable.

"And Simon answering said unto him, Master, we have toiled all the night, and have taken nothing: nevertheless at thy word I will let down the net."
- Luke 5:5

If God's word has no place in your heart real courage is not in place. But when you act based on the word of God that is grounded and rooted in your heart, Courage will rise to help you give answers to the conflicts of life.

REMEMBER

- One man with courage is greater than a majority that lacks courage.

- Courage is acting on a need greater than self.
- All true champions are men of courage.
- If courage is not in place, ultimate victory is elusive.
- Winners take courage to make decisions.
- Where there is no courage fear takes over.
- God respects the courage of champions.
- The reality of God's presence is the greatest source of good courage.

CHAPTER 10

Winners Are Men Of Vision

"To have sight without vision is worse than being born blind."
- Unknown

Vision breeds creative changes. A discovery of God's plan as it relates to you, is what we call vision. Vision is the mystery behind the triumph of every successful man on this planet. No man ever saw victory without seeing vision. Someone defined vision as foresight with insight based on hindsight.

A discovery of Gods plan as it relates to you is what we call visions.

But according to Stephen Covey:

"Vision means to begin with the end in mind."

Vision is superior to Ambition. Ambition is what you want done. Vision is what God wants you to do. So, God's purpose is started by vision.

"I will stand upon my watch, and set me upon the tower, and will watch to see what he will say unto me, and what I shall answer when I am reproved."
- Habakkuk 2:1

Some people go into business or projects without discovering God's set plan for their lives. No wonder there are many failures around. Men who succeed are men who not only have discovered God's plan for their lives, but also pursued such plans. Winners don't embark on a journey God has not sent them. They spend time to know his Ways and acts.

> "He made known his ways unto Moses, his acts unto the children of Israel."
> - Psalms 103:7

HOW VISION IS ACQUIRED AND PURSUED

> "I will stand upon my watch, and set me upon the tower, and will watch to see what he will say unto me, and what I shall answer when I am reproved.
> And the Lord answered me, and said, write the vision, and make it plain upon tables, that he may run that readeth it.
> **For the vision is yet for an appointed time, but at the end it shall speak, and not lie: though it tarry, wait for it; because it will surely come, it will not tarry.**
> **Behold, his soul, which is lifted up, is not upright in him: but the just shall live by his faith."**
> - Habakkuk 2: 1-4

The first thing winners do to acquire vision is to:

i.   ***Stand upon their watch:*** You have to separate yourself from the crowd. Stand as an individual because you are peculiar, you are different from the rest. So, choose to stand differently. Joshua, Caleb and Elisha were examples of men who chose to be different. They stood alone in faith and acquired their vision.

ii. **_Watching_:** Vision can be born in the place of prayer and watching. Prayer gives grace for vision. Watching gives direction and alertness to vision. When prayer gives birth to vision, watching protects it from being derailed.

iii. **_Winners write down their vision_:** A vision not written down can be forgotten. Winners understand that the faintest pencil is sharper than the sharpest brain. So they write down the vision and make it plain, precise and readable. Jesus was writing on the ground when a woman caught in adultery was brought to him. When he rose up and spoke, the crowd disappeared. Obviously, he was receiving wisdom from God and writing them down.

iv. **_Run with the vision_:** Once a vision is acquired and documented, it is now time to work towards its attainment. It involves stretching yourself to fulfill every aspect of the vision. Activities of the vision become a daily routine. You Work daily to become your expectation. This is a Winning habit. Action is put into a vision. This time calls for discipline.

"And every man that striveth for the mastery is temperate in all things. Now they do it to obtain a Corruptible crown; but we an incorruptible."
- 1 Corinthians 9:25

"Where there is no vision [no redemptive revelations of God], the people perish; but he who keeps the law [of God, which includes that of man], blessed, happy, fortunate

[and enviable] is he."
- Proverbs 29:18 (Amplified)

v.   ***Understanding the appointed time***: Time is important to any vision. Miss the time for your visitation and you sign in for frustration. A timeless vision is unachievable vision. Patience is also needed since faith and patience are two sides of the same coin in the fulfillment of vision.

WINNERS GET AT ATTENTION THROUGH VISION

Men who command attention are men of vision. When you are focused on the attainment of a worthwhile goal through vision, you attract attention. Blind Bartimaeus in Mark 10:40-55 got the attention of Jesus Christ when he persisted to achieve his vision.

Vision is a strong motivator. It challenges and helps to bring out the best in the lives or all that hook on to it. In Genesis Chapter 37, we see how Joseph received a delivery of vision. At age seventeen, God filled him with visions of his destiny:
He discovered destiny.

This vision later became a moderating and motivating factor in his life. Not even the likes of Potiphar's wife could distract him from his vision. He knew what was ahead. Nothing else was able to push him off his focus. Joseph's eventual elevation to the position of the most powerful ruler in a foreign land — Egypt, is an eloquent testimony of the power of vision.

Vision plus action equals realization
- E. A. Adeboye

REMEMBER

- A discovery of God's plans as it pertains to you is what we call vision.
- No man ever saw victory without seeing vision.
- Vision is superior to ambition.
- Vision can be born in the place of prayer and watching.
- When prayer gives birth to vision, watching protects it from being derailed.
- A timeless vision is an unachievable vision.

CHAPTER 11

Winners Avoid Undue Exposure

We are in the age of Internet; The age of information explosion. The age of information without borders. And this has its good and ugly sides.

While not disputing the essence of exposure which has helped the growth of various nations, economies and people. One must be on guard against undue exposure that leads to failure, moral decadence and ultimate defeat in the hands of the enemy of our lives — the devil.

> *If treasures are exposed to the enemy, captivity is inevitable.*

One must be Wise not to open up to things and people that are out to destroy us. Mind what you watch on television. Beware of what you read. Select those you expose your life and business to. There are those who will laugh with you in the open, but will kill you in secret. Don't be a talkative.

Mind those you take counsel from..

A good illustration of undue exposure is the life of Hezekiah in Isaiah 39:1 - 4.

"At that time Merodach - baladan, the son of Baladan, king
of Babylon, sent letters and presents to Hezekiah: for he
had heard that he had been sick, and was recovered.

And Hezekiah was glad of them, and shewed them the
house of his precious things, the silver, and the gold, and
the spices, and the precious ointments, and the house of his
armour, and all that was found in his treasures: there was
nothing in his house, nor in all his dominion, that Hezekiah
shewed them not.

Then came Isaiah the prophet unto King Hezekiah, and
said unto him, What said these men? And from whence
came they unto thee? And Hezekiah said they are come
from afar country unto me even from Babylon.

Then said he what have they seen in thy house? And Hezekiah answered, All that is in my house have they seen:
There is nothing among my treasure that I have not shewed
them."

Hezekiah had just received healing and more years to his life by
God's divine grace. Many people including his enemies came to
congratulate him. During this period Hezekiah displayed all his
treasures to the people of Babylon He exposed himself to his enemies.

Hear what God said to him by the mouth of Isaiah

"Then said Isaiah unto Hezekiah, Hear the word of the
Lord of Host: Behold, the days come, that all that is in thine
house, and that which thy father has laid up in store until
this day, shall be carried into Babylon: nothing shall be left,
saith the Lord.

And from thy sons which shall issue from thee, which thou
shall beget, shall they take away; and they shall be eunuchs
in the palace of the king of Babylon.

Then said Hezekiah unto Isaiah, Good is the word of the
Lord, which thou has spoken. He said moreover, there shall
be peace and truth in my days."
- Isaiah 39 : 5 -8

If we expose our treasures to the enemy, Captivity is inevitable. In the African continent, over-celebration of wedding ceremonies, naming ceremonies and burial ceremonies is the order of the day. Many families have during such occasions opened up themselves to untold hardship. Some have become barren and others penniless due to an exposure of their lives to the enemy.

In celebrating your successes, be on guard. Every action of a Winner must be prayerfully thought out. David exposed the Israelites by numbering them. As soon as he numbered the children of Israel, death set in and many died.
So, be on guard to reach your goal. Over exposure can be over-expensive. Undue exposure leads to undue expenses.

REMEMBER

- One must be wise not to open up to things that are out to destroy us.

- Select those who you expose your life and business to.
- If your treasures are exposed to the enemy, captivity is inevitable.
- Every action of a winner must be prayerfully thought out.

- Undue exposure leads to undue expenses.

CHAPTER 12

Winners Bring Solutions To Problems

Had he not interpreted and given solutions to the problems of Pharaoh's dream, Joseph would never have tasted rulership in Egypt. He solved Pharaoh's problem and Pharaoh solved his own.

"And Pharaoh said unto Joseph, Forasmuch as God has shewed thee all this, there is none so discrete and wise as thou art: Thou shall be over my house, and according unto thy word shall all my people be ruled: only in the throne will I be greater than thou. And Pharaoh said unto Joseph See I have set thee over all the land of Egypt."
- Genesis 41: 39 – 41

Winners learn how to empower others to succeed.

Daniel's elevation also came to him because he was a problem solver. Every successful businessman solves problems for his clients. Doctors solve health problems. Pastors solve spiritual problems.

Electricians solve electrical problems. If you are not a problem solver, you are a problem giver. And no one tastes success by giving people more problems. If you don't give others what they need, they won't give you what you need.

You Are An Answer

God made you a solution to some needs. Locate those who needs you. Meet their needs and you will become successful.

Elijah was in need of an Elisha. Elisha could not have made it without Elijah. Elisha met Elijah's need and Elijah met Elisha's need. Whoever is not ready to be an answer to other's problems is not ready for success in life.

> *"We then who are strong ought to bear the infirmities of the weak, and not to please ourselves. Let every one of us please his neighbour for his good to edification. For even*
> *Christ pleased not himself: but, as it is written, The reproaches of them that reproached thee fell on me."*
> *- Romans 15: 1 - 3*

Winners seek problems they have solutions to. They seek to find those who need their help. They identify clearly what they have to offer to others.

You are a solution going somewhere to happen. You are the only you in the universe. There is something unique about you. God has packaged some answers in you. So, don't be a liability in God's Kingdom. You are an answer.

> *"Let every man abide in the same calling wherein he was called."*
> *- Corinthians 7: 20*

Abide where God has called you to work. You are working for yourself by working for God. The greatest secret of winning God's favor is by winning others for God.

There are problems you can solve for this dying world: You can bring hope to the hopeless, bring life to the dying, bring food to the hungry, bring joy to the sorrowful, bring peace to the troubled, bring clothes to the naked, light to those in darkness. This is the way to a truly fulfilled life.

Anything that will not bring solution to others will never bring you success. If you don't help others to win, you are the greatest looser.

Winners Empower Others

Winners learn how to empower others to succeed. Jesus said:

> *"... Follow me and I will make you..."*
> *- Matthew 4: 19*

If you are already a problem to the society, allow God to make you a solution. You must bring meaning into people's lives for you to be meaningful at all. Help to develop people thereby enabling them to be rightly positioned for progress.

REMEMBER

- If you don't give others what they need, they won't give you what you need.
- God made you a solution to some needs.
- God has put some gifts and talents in you.

- If you don't help others to win, you are the greatest looser.

- Winners learn how to transfer and empower others to succeed.

- The greatest secret of winning is by winning others for God.

- Help to develop people therefore enabling them to be rightly positioned for progress

CHAPTER 13

Winners Are Finishers

Many people start on a project but only few see the project through to the end. A Winner is the one who has the courage to finish what he has started. He works to see the end of any beginning.

It is not just enough to start. One must attempt to finish what he has started inspite of the difficulties put on the way.

Jesus is called the Alfa and Omega, the beginning and the end. God never starts what he cannot finish.

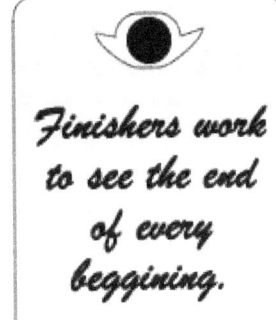

> *"Being confident of this that he who began a good work in you will perform it until the day of Christ."*
> *- Philippians 1 : 6*

Jesus is called a finisher. He endured shame because of the joy of victory. He endured the cross to see the solution of sin in humanity.

> *"Looking unto Jesus the author and finisher of our faith, who for the joy that was set before him, endured the cross, despising the shame, and is set down at the right hand of the throne of God".*
> *- Romans 12: 2*

He completed every aspect of the Work of salvation. No wonder he cried on the cross:

> *"... It is finished. "*
> *-John 19: 3*

Earlier in his prayer for the saints Jesus said:

> *"I have glorified thee on earth: I have finished the work which thou gavest me to do."*
> *-John 17 : 4*

It is not just enough to do the will of God; we must also finish the work we are given to perform.

There is always a battle to fight in order to finish what one has started. Such a fight Paul calls the good fight.
A good fight is the fight that brings good success; A war that makes you a Winner.

REMEMBER

- A good fight is the fight that brings success; a war that makes you a winner.

- A winner is one who has the courage to finish what he has started.

- There is always a battle to fight in order to finish what one has started.

- It is not just enough to do the will of God, we must also finish the work we are given to perform.

CHAPTER 14

Winners Are Men Of Great Passion

"When you want knowledge as much as you want air, you will get it. "
- Socrates

Passion breeds enthusiasm and it is the first step to achieving any worthwhile goal in life. Passion is a strong, deep feeling of either love or hatred for something. Godly passion signs you on for progress in every area of life. Nothing significant was ever achieved without passion.

"Whatsoever thy hand findeth to do, do it with thy might; for there is no work, nor device, nor knowledge, nor wisdom in the grave wither thou goest. "
- Proverbs 9 : 10

As Fuel for the will, passion enlarges mans will power.

As fuel for the will, Passion enlarges man's willpower. Just as small fire produces little heat, weak desires bring weak results. Winners are aware that passion can make ordinary people great people. Passion is power.

A passion for excellence brings success. Jesus was a passionate man. The passion for His purpose led him to death and brought us salvation.

"For God so loved the world, that he gave his only begotten son, that whosoever believeth in him should not perish but have everlasting life."
- John 3 : 16

That is why a relationship with Christ ignites divine passion for excellence in man. You can't ignite fire if you don't have it burning in you. When the fire of passion is lost, your movement to relevance is terminated. If you have lost the fire of passion for success, get around Jesus. He is a fire lighter.

No passion, no salvation. Passion is what makes HUMANITY and DIVINITY to kiss in Christ. Passion never fails; it gives strength at the face of weakness.

"If you follow your passion instead of others' perceptions, you can't help becoming a more dedicated, productive person. This increases your ability to impact others. In the end, your passion will have more influence than your personality. "
- J. C. Maxwell

So, find something that consumes you; something you love; something worth living for, and build your life around it.
This is the way to winning.

The key to attainment in any business venture is purposeful passion. It is impossible to achieve true recognition in any field of endeavor without it. What makes men achieve the incredible is passion.

How To Develop Passion

1. Spend time to think and work on something of deep interest to you.

2. Set a goal for the achievement of your area of interest. Count the cost and be ready to pay the price.

3. Get inspiration for action in that area. Action drives away fear. Action develops courage.

4. Reverence your goal. Believe you can achieve it. Give it all it takes.

5. Avoid distractions of destiny. Have focus and be single minded.

6. Learn all you can about the business. Be open to new ideas.

7. Have the end reward in mind. Think daily about the honour the achievement of the goal will bring to your life.

"I don't mean to say I am perfect. I have not learnt all I should even yet, but I keep working toward that day when I will finally be all that Christ saved me for and wants me to be.

... But I am bringing all my energies to bear on this one thing: Forgetting the past and looking to what lies ahead, I strain to reach the end of the race and receive the price for which God is calling us up to heaven because of what Christ did for us. "
- Philippians 3: 12 - 14 (TLB)

REMEMBER

- Passion breeds enthusiasm. Passion is power.

- Nothing significant was ever achieved without passion.

- Passion is what makes men achieve the incredible.

- When the fire of passion is lost, your movement to relevance is terminated.

- If you have lost the fire of passion get around Jesus.

- Passion never fails, it gives strength at the face of weakness.

CHAPTER 15

Winners Agree And Walk With God

Good success is knowing God's will and doing it. Winners come to terms with this divine fact. They learn to walk in agreement with God's ordained pattern of events. They meditate day and night on God's word. They believe that God is always right. And that for things to be right God's rules must be followed.

Winners recognize that God is the author and finisher of every good venture. So they learn to follow Him.

Having the right partnership enhances progress.

> *"Except the Lord builds the house they labour in vain that build it."*
> *- Psalms 127 : 1*

God is the best business partner anyone can ever have. Whatever He says, He has the power to perform.

> *"God is not a man that He should lie; neither the son of man that he should repent: hath he said, and shall not do it?*
> *Or has he spoken, and shall he not make it good."*
> *- Numbers 23 : 19*

> *"And also the strength of Israel will not lie nor repent: for*

he is not a man that he should repent."
- l Samuel 15 : 29

Winners Avoid Being Alone

God never intends that man be alone. He demonstrated this at the beginning of creation by making a help meet for man.

> *"And the Lord God said it is not good (sufficient, satisfactory) that man should be alone: I will make him a helper meet (suitable, adapted, completing) for him."*
> *- Genesis 2 : 18 (Amplified)*

Man needs a partner to succeed in every great endeavor: so don't be alone. Give and accept help, especially God's help. The rich needs help the poor needs help. God and you could form an unbeatable team.

> *"With God nothing shall be impossible."*
> *- Luke 1: 37*

Our fathers of faith made success of their sojourn on earth because they struck a perfect partnership with God. You can draw inspiration from the following lives.

> *JOSEPH*
> *"And the Lord was with Joseph, and he was a prosperous man; and he was in the house of his master the Egyptian. But the Lord was with Joseph, and showed him mercy, and gave him favor in the sight of the keeper of the prison."*
> *- Genesis 39:2, 21*
>
> *SAMUEL*
> *"And Samuel grew, and the Lord was with him, and he did*

not let his words fall to the ground."
- I Samuel 3: 19

DAVID
"And David went on, and grew great, and the Lord God of Host was with him.
- 2 Samuel 5: 10

SOLOMON
"And Solomon the son of David was strengthened in his kingdom and the Lord his God was with him and magnified him exceedingly. "
- 2 Chronicles 1: 1

PAUL
"Notwithstanding the Lord stood with me, and strengthened me; that by me the preaching might be fully known, and that all the Gentiles might hear: and I was delivered out of the mouth of the lion."
- 2 Timothy 4 : 17

JESUS
"How God anointed Jesus of Nazareth with the Holy Ghost and with power: who went about doing good, healing all that were oppressed of the devil: for God was with him."
- Acts 10 : 38

"The same came to Jesus at night and said unto him, Rabbi, we know that thou art a teacher come from God: for no one can do these miracles that thou doest except God be with him."
-John 3 : 2

You can see that these great men made it to the top because God was with them in partnership. Having the right partnership enhances progress. Responsibilities are shared.

The burden is less, greater results than what a single individual can achieve become possible. The ability and strength of the team members are released for the attainment of set goals.

Winners Carry God's Presence

To be able to carry God's presents, you must carry His presence. This is because by strength shall no man prevail in the battles of life.

> *"He will keep the feet of his saints, and the wicked shall be silent in darkness; for by strength shall no man prevail. "*
> *-1 Samuel 2: 9*

Winners have an understanding that if God is not there, his goods will not be there. So they carry his presence in whatsoever they do. Nothing withstands God's presence.

> *"... If God be for us, who can be against us?"*
> *- Romans 8: 31*

God's presence renders your enemies helpless. Moses knew that God's presence is vital in winning the battles of life.
Hear him:

> *"And He said, My presence shall go with thee, and I will give thee rest. And he said unto him, If thy presence go not with me, carry us not up hence."*
> *- Exodus 33: 14 - 15*

The presence of God is what makes the lives of true winners radiate joy when others are groaning.

> *"Thou wilt shew me the path of life: in thy presence is fullness of joy; at thy right hand there are pleasures forever*

more. "
- *Psalms 16: 11*

Whoever desires success or increase in any endeavor, must learn to carry His presence. It is God that gives increase.

> *"I have planted, Apollos watered; but God gave the increase. "*
> - *l Corinthians 3: 6*

God's presence attracts success. You can't be a looser if God is there. If you put God first all other things will follow.

> *"But seek ye first the kingdom of God, and his righteousness; and all these things shall be added unto you."*
> - *Matthew 6: 33*

No matter how hard you work, without God's assistance it amounts to nothing.

> *"But by the grace of God I am what I am: and his grace which was bestowed upon me was not in vain... "*
> **-1 Corinthians 15 : 10**

> *" For without me you can do nothing."*
> - *John 15: 5*

Until the man on top takes you to the top, you remain at the bottom.

> *"For promotion cometh neither from the East, nor from the West, nor from the South. But God is the judge: he putteth down one, and setteth up another. "*
> - *Psalms 75: 6 - 7*

Any help from man to you is because God desires to help you. God is the one that sends men to help you.

> *"And David went out to meet them, and answered and said unto them, If ye be come peaceably unto me to help me, mine heart shall be knit unto you: but if ye be come to betray me to mine enemies, seeing there is no wrong in mine hands, the God of our fathers look thereon, and rebuke it. Then the spirit came upon Amasai, who was chief of the captains, and he said, Thine are we, David, and on thy side, thou son of Jesse: peace, peace be unto thee, and peace be to thine helpers; for thy God helpeth thee. Then David received them and made them captains of the band. "*
> *- I Chronicles 12 : 16 - 18*

> *"And God helped him against the Philistines, and against the Arabians that dwelt in*
> *Gur-baal, and the Mehunims.*
> *… And he made in Jerusalem engines, in vented by cunning men, to be on the towers and upon the bulwarks, to shoot arrows and great stones withal. And his name spread far abroad; for he was marvelously helped, till he was strong. "*
> *- 2 Chronicles 26 : 7, 15*

Help from above is what lifts men. The help from above is above all others. Those who seek help from below when help from above is available end up as mediocre. God is a very present help in time of need. Winners are those .who have come to understand that everything great is a product of grace.

REMEMBER

- Winners learn to walk in agreement with God's ordained pattern of events.

- Winners learn to give and accept help, especially God's help.

- God is the best business partner anyone could ever have

- Having the right partnership enhances progress.

- If you put God first all other things will follow.

- Any help from man to you is because God helps you.

- Winners are those who know that everything great is a product of grace.

CHAPTER 16

Winning Involves Preparation

"So Jotham became mighty, because he prepared his ways before the Lord his God."
- 2 Chronicles 27: 6

Preparation is the first step to partaking in the supernatural and it is the greatest determinant to winning. It is only what you prepare for that you can partake of. If you don't prepare for success you won't partake in success.

Preparation precedes promotion. In actual sense, the difference between winning and loosing is in adequate preparation. Champions become winners through their daily preparation and routine activities. You don't become a boxing champion in the ring. Champions only earn recognition in the ring.

When preparation meets with God given opportunity, success happens. No good preparation, no good performance.

Sluggards don't get anywhere because they don't prepare for anywhere. And because victory is prepared for, Winners don't worry about the future, they prepare for the future.

> *"Go to the ant, thou sluggarrl; consider her ways and be wise: which having no guide, overseer or ruler, provideth her meat in the summer, and gathereth her food in the harvest."*
> *- Proverbs 6: 6 - 8*

Preparation precedes possession. In other Words if you are not prepared, you cannot possess. You are ready for only what you have prepared for. God is available to be your guide in preparing for the future. The ants have no guide yet they have learnt the art of preparation for the future.
Adequate preparation is practical Wisdom in action. If you fail to prepare, you have already prepared to fail.

The act of preparation is to get you ready for a specific purpose. Success gotten by surprise will disappear by surprise.

Preparation involves training and acquiring knowledge. You can hardly prosper in something you are not prepared for.
Only fools expect success without adequate preparation.

If you don't prepare you will never make progress in life. You can see how long it takes to train a medical doctor or an engineer. Every good success requires a period of preparation.

Prosperity Is Prepared For

You prepare for good by doing what is right at the right time. Even prosperity is prepared for. Jotham started preparing for greatness at an early age. The bible says:

> *"And he did that which was right in the sight of the Lord."*
> *- 2 Chronicles 27 : 2*

Jotham attained greatness when he prepared his way before the

Lord. He knew that the foundation for every success starts with God.

Establish the right relationship with God early in life. Any preparation that leaves God out of the scheme of things is doomed to fail. The future belongs to those who prepare for it in God.

> *"And he did evil, because he prepared not his heart to seek the Lord. "*
> *- 2Chronicles 12 : 14*

Rehoboam failed as a king because he did not prepare his heart to seek God. Miracles will always happen, but only those who are prepared will receive.

REMEMBER

- It is only what you prepare for that you can partake of

- Champions become winners through their daily preparation and routine activities.

- No good preparation, no good performance.

- Sluggards don't get anywhere because they don't prepare for anywhere.

- Preparation precedes possession.

- Success gotten by surprise will disappear by surprise.

- Only fools expect success without adequate preparation.

- The future belongs to those who prepare for it in God.

CHAPTER 17

Winners Are Good Planners

"For which of you, intending to build a tower sitteth not down first, and counteth the cost, whether he have sufficient to finish it?"
- Luke 14:28

"Commit to the Lord whatever you do, and your plans will succeed."
- Proverbs 16: 3 (NIV)

A major determinant of winners is planning. God the creator of all things is a planner. All of His successes are due to meticulous planning and execution. No Wonder God never fails.

If success is the goal, planning must be good.

The common saying that "if you fail to plan, you have planned to fail" is a Wise if A declaration. Poor results come from poor planning.

A plan is a written arrangement of actions vital to the achievement of a desired goal. Anyone aiming to succeed must first sit down to draw up a plan. It is the starting point of any worthwhile venture. You are walking your way into avoidable problems if you start any enterprise without good planning. Planning is the difference between letting it happen and enabling it happen. Good planning helps us to set our priorities thereby enhancing the doing of the right thing at the right time. Tasks are broken into stages. Strategies are then marked out for their achievements.

So plan your Way to the top and nothing can stop you with God on your side.

If success is the goal, planning must be good. No planning, No profit.

Planning Increases Effectiveness

> *"Any enterprise is built by wise planning, becomes strong through common sense and profits wonderfully by keeping abreast of the facts."*
> *- Proverb 24:5-4 (TLB)*

A planned life is a goal-oriented life. It is difficult to be effective in any endeavor without adequate planning. Planning increases effectiveness.

Those who will through planning identify the key roles and invest the scarce resources in those areas, are those who will always make it to the top of the success ladder.

Plan and do what you have planned. If you don't do what you have planned, you will follow other people's plans. And that is not the path of Winners.

Winners Plan To Be what God Says They Are

God reckons us to be more than conquerors. Not just conquerors but more than conquerors.

> *"Nay, in all these things we are more than conquerors*

through him that loved us."
- Romans 8:37

Winners realize the great things they can achieve through Christ. So, they plan towards extraordinary breakthrough. This is the root to great inventions and monumental accomplishments. They know that with God nothing shall he impossible. They look at problems on the face and proffer solutions through wise planning.

They are quite aware of what the Holy Scriptures say:

"Ye are of God, little children, and have overcome them: because greater is he that is in you, than he that is in the world"
- l John 4:4

In planning for the achievement of their desires, they ask and receive; they seek and find. In the life of true winners, there is no day without a plan to overcome. They have the faith that overcomes the World and they win where others fail. Winners refuse to over analyze circumstances and situations in their plans. They know that too much analysis leads to paralysis. Failure is inevitable if faith is not given its proper place.

Good success is knowing the will of God and doing it.

REMEMBER

- The success of winners depends on meticulous planning and execution.
- Planning is the difference between letting it happen and enabling it happen.
- Planning increases effectiveness.

- If you don't do what you have planned, you will follow other people's plans.
- Winners refuse to over analyze circumstances in their plans.
- Failure is inevitable if faith is not given its proper place.
- Good success is knowing the will of God and doing it.
- Winners look at problems on the face and proffer solutions.

CHAPTER 18

Winning Involves Dreaming Big

Dreamers are history makers. No big dream, no big deal and the substance of great accomplishments, are great dreams. The late Martin Luther King of America had a dream In April 30, 1968 the day before his assassination, he said and l quote:

> *"I have a dream. I have looked over and I have seen the promise land. I may not get there with you, but I want to know that we as a people will get to the promise land."*

Today that dream is being achieved. The blacks in America are gradually taking their proper place.

Dreams are driving forces of achievement.

A dream is the mental picture of your given destiny. The future belongs to men who believe in the beauty of their God given dream. What you dream about, you can become. What you see, you become. So, seize your dream and don't let it disappear.

Joseph was a man who held on to his dream until it was actualized.

> *"And he said unto them, Hear, I pray you, this dream which I have dreamed: For, behold, we were binding sheaves in the field, and, lo, my sheaves arose, and also stood upright;*

and, behold, your sheaves also stood round about, and made obeisance to my sheaf
And his brethren said unto him, Shall thou indeed reign over us? Or shall thou indeed have dominion over us? And they hated him yet the more for his dreams, and for his words.
- Genesis 37: 6 - 8

People may hate you and your dreams. But they cannot halt your dreams except you let them. Joseph became the leader in Egypt because he had the dream to become such. From his youth, he saw others bowing before him.

A dream is something you look forward to achieving in the future. No man achieves anything if he goes through life without a dream. Dreams are the driving force of achievement.

Let your dreams dominate your direction. You must have an idea of where you are going before you can get there. A dream opens the lid. That is why the most wretched people on earth are those who have lost the ability to dream.

However, dreams alone will not get you there. Too many people are day dreaming, having big ideas but never taking any seriously. Acting on your success dream gives you dominion over failure.

According to T. E. Lawrence:

"All people dream but not equally. Those who dream by night in the dusty recesses of their mind wake up in the day to find it was vanity. But the dreamers of the day are dangerous people. For they might act their dreams with open eyes to make it possible."

Avoid Dream Destroyers

Dare to dream big, dare to see your dream come to pass. There are many dream destroyers hanging around to frustrate every God given dream. Winners are those who avoid dream destroyers.

Self-sufficiency is one of those enemies of our dreams.
When a man is held up in self- sufficiency and maintenance of the status quo, no dream can be realized. And this state must be avoided like a plague in order to realize the beautiful dreams that will come our Way.

Impossibility thinking and talking can kill good dreams. If with God all things are possible, all things are equally possible with man that has God on his side. With more

Knowledge, determination and faith every seeming impossible situation melts into possibility.

Exaggerations and exaggerators also exacerbate problems on the Way of a dreamer. Small challenges can be magnified to be huge impenetrable obstacles through the lens of exaggerations. But re-member, what you can dream, you can do. Exaggerations can cost you the Promised Land.

Kingdom dreams are sustained by the enabling power of the Holy Spirit. Stay with him and he will make your dreams stay.

REMEMBER

- Dreamers are history makers.
- No big dream, no big deal.
- The future belongs to men who believe in their God given dream.
- Acting on your success dream gives you dominion over failure.
- People cannot halt your dreams unless you let them.
- Impossibility thinking and can kill good dreams.
- All things are possible with a man that has God on his side.
- Kingdom dreams are sustained by the power of the Holy Ghost.

CHAPTER 19

Winners Are Victors By Choice

"I have set before thee life and death, blessing and cursing, therefore choose life, that both thou and thy seed may live."
- Deuteronomy 3: 19

The most important ability God has given man, is the ability to choose. Man is allowed to make his choice. What anyone becomes in life depends on the choices he makes.

In our daily sojourn on earth, life and death, success and failure, stare us in the face. The one we choose is the one we experience. Your actions show the choice you have made.

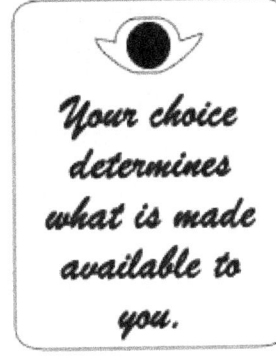

Your choice determines what is made available to you.

Your words show God the choice you have made. Your manner of life shows your choice.

Beloved you can choose life *"that both thou and thy seed may live."* What you choose determines your future and that of your seed. You can see how weighty the matter is.

Power Is Available

"But as many as received him to them gave he power to become the sons of God..."
- John 1 : 12

Your choice determines what is made available to you. There is power to do good and it is the power for outstanding success in life, the power of sonship with God. This enormous power is made available to those whose choice is life, who have received and accepted Jesus Christ as Lord and Saviour.

With this power you are granted the legal right, privilege and authority to the omnipotent power of God.
There is also the power to do evil. Those who refuse the choice of life have automatic access to this power. The devil is evil; he makes those who refuse life evil merchants.

The choice of life brings an anointing to do good. Every Son of God is consecrated to propagate good things. An inborn ability for doing good radiates in them by reason of the Holy Ghost.

In this business, what you become in life depends on how you choose to use this God given power. Jesus went about utilizing this power to heal the sick, to deliver the oppressed of the devil and to spread good tidings.

Success in life never eludes those who make good use of this power. It forcefully procures good and healthy living for them that know what they have. Herein lies wisdom.

History abounds with people who refused to be content with the situation life fostered on them. They chose to change inspite of all odds. You can be one of them, but first, make a choice of life; a choice to be victorious.

Winners Choose To Obtain God's Promises

> *"That ye be not slothful, but followers of them who through faith and patience inherit the promises."*
> *- Hebrews 6 : 12*

We are admonished to follow the footsteps of those who succeeded in the race of life. They inherited the promises of God for their lives in their time. They chose to be victorious.

God will oblige you according to your choice. He won't force anything on you. The bible is replete with examples of people that chose to be victorious: Paul in Acts 14 : 19 - 20 was stoned to death but chose to live. He came back to life in the same city where he had been killed. But Stephen cried to the Lord to receive his spirit when the first stone landed on him. And the Lord received him out of this world.

> *"And they stoned Stephen, calling upon God, and saying, Lord Jesus receive my spirit."*
> *- Acts 7: 59*

A centurion informed Jesus of his sick servant. Jesus obliged to come and heal him at home. The centurion refused and chose instead that Jesus speak the word only. Jesus did and the servant was healed instantly.

> *"And Jesus said unto him, I will come and heal him. The centurion answered and said, Lord, I am not worthy that thou shouldest come under my roof: but speak the word only, and my servant shall be healed. "*
> *- Matthew 8 : 7 - 8*

Jairus, a ruler in the synagogue, on his part chose to have Jesus come to his house to heal his daughter. The Woman with the issue of blood preferred a touch on Jesus for her healing. Jesus obliged according to the various choices.
Your choice has a role to play in how and what you receive.

What You Choose Is What You Get

"And what more shall I say? For time will fail me to tell of Gideon, and of Barak, and of Samson, and of Jephthah; of David also, and Samuel, and of the prophets:

Who through faith subdued kingdoms, wrought righteousness, obtained promises, stopped the mouths of lions, Quenched the violence of fire, escaped the edge of the sword, out of weaknesses were made strong, waxed valiant in fight, turned to flight the armies of the aliens.

Women received their dead raised to life again: and others were tortured, not accepting deliverance; that they might obtain a better resurrection:

And others had trials of cruel mocking and scourgings, yea, moreover of bonds and imprisonment:

They were stoned they were sawn asunder, were tempted, were slain with the sword: they wandered about in sheepskins and goatskins; being destitute, afflicted, tormented;

(Of whom the world was not worthy ') they wandered in deserts, and in mountains, and in dens and caves of the earth.

And these all, having obtained a good report through faith, received not the promise."

- Hebrews 11 : 32 - 39

There are two groups of men of faith as we see in the scriptures above. One group obtained the promises of God for their lives and the other group after allowing all kinds of Suffering obtained only a good report.

In the first group we find Gideon (Judges 6: 1 - 8, 35); Barak (Judges 4:1 - 5, 31); Samson (Judges 13: 1-16, 31): Jephthah (Judges 11 : I - 15); David (1 Samuel 17: 32 - 51; 23: 2, 11; 2 Samuel 3: 18; 7: 1 - 17; 8: 1 - 3; 12: 16 - 24) e.t.c.

They subdued kingdoms, brought righteousness, obtained promises, closed the mouths of lions, extinguished the power of raging tires, and escaped the edge of the sword.

Then we have the second group of men of faith that the bible refers to as others. And we know that it includes Stephen (Acts 6-7); John the Baptist (Matthew 1 - 1 l) and many others.

The Bible says they were stoned to death, slain with the sword, wandered about in sheepskins and goatskins, were afflicted and tormented but not accepting deliverance. They obtained a good report but did not obtain the promised blessings.

One group obtained the promised blessings, the other group despite refusing deliverance obtained only a good report and not the promise. Friends, you can choose which of the group you want to emulate.

Choose between good report and promised blessings. I have chosen to obtain the promised blessings. Promised blessings include a good report. But a good report does not include obtaining promised blessings.

REMEMBER

- Your manner of life shows your choice.
- Your choice determines your future and that of your seed.

- God obliges you according to your choice.

- The choice of life brings an anointing to do good.

- Choose the promised blessings; it includes a good report.

BOOKS BY THIS AUTHOR

Strategic Living: Discover The Golden Keys To Living Well And Finishing Well

A book foreword by Dr. Myles Munroe, this book shows you the right ways to strategically position
yourself

Life Lessons From The Ants

In the book of the life lessons from the Ants, the writer describes how God is speaking to the
sluggard-this refers to one who is lazy, idle, careless, sticks to nothing, minds no business and brings
nothing to pass.

Irresistible Leader

IRRESISTIBLE LEADER, a book that would show you what it takes to become irresistible, lead irresistibly,
living a high definition life, principles from jesus' life, principles of leading irresistibly and many
more

The Money Question: The Christian And Money

The Money Question.This book helps dismiss the fact and mystery about money and Christianity. Most
Christians have related Christianity to poverty and riches to covetousness; but to the contrary Jesus
uses money as a symbol to explaining a lot of fact and figures about "heaven and earth" and
"relationship between the heavenly father and us".If we are called

Priest and Kings, meaning we are here
to reign and also worship HIM, we as kings are not to be poor in spirit, health and physical things.The
money question also shades more light on how to perceive money and relate it to your Christian faith.

Winning Habits: Another Bestseller From The Author Of Achieving Success

Winning Habits is a book that is meant to teach us how to succeed and be perpetual winners.

123 Nuggets For Great Achievements: From The Author Of Winning Habits

In 123 Nuggets for Great Achievements, bestselling author, Peter Amenkhienan has again capture truth
that will inspire you to leave above average, act your best and be your best in all that you do. Every
page is loaded with nuggets of wisdom, packaged to make the simple wise and even wiser.Consider
these:·It is the leading of God that makes you a progressive leader on earth·Dominion is impossible
without wisdom·The courage to take risk is the key to success·If your treasures are exposed to the
enemy, captivity is inevitable·You need a big mouth to control a big territory ·If you refuse to die, no
man will bury you·No one will befriend you if you have nothing to offer

Limitless Leadership

Limitless Leadership

Advancing Through Adversities

Advancing or making progress is a function of how we handle adversity: while some people crash with
every difficult situation, some other have learnt to use their storms to soar to great heights. you can
advance inspite of the negative circumstances of life.

You can achieve what you set out to achieve. In this book, the author has packaged great insight and
wisdom to put you on the winning side of life. You are not meant to be a victim. You can advance through
that adversity.

Prosperity Principles

You don't have to be poor. Prosperity is available, it is attainable, and also achievable. It operates
on basic principles anyone can easily put to work.
 Peter Amenkhienan has clearly enumerated these principles with a glossary of Bible references that
makes it clear and simple for all to read.

Living Above Limitations

Advancing or making progress is a function of how we handle adversity. While some people crash with every difficult situation, some others have learnt to use their storms to soar to great heights. You can advance inspite of the negative circumstance of life.
 You can achieve what you set out to achieve. In this book, the author has packaged great insights and wisdom to put you on the winning side of life. You are not meant to be a victim. You can advance through that adversity.

Living Above Limitations

You don't have to be limited in life. You don't have to allow negative circumstance to force you to submission. You can soar like the eagle, and operate in the realm of high flier.
 This dynamic book by Peter Amenkhienan will change your life forever. With step by step guidelines and powerful scriptural principles, Pastor Peter will ignite your passion for excellence and challenge you to live above limitations. This book contains the secrets of triumphant living.

Achieving Success

Peter Amenkhienen, in this book presents to you the pathfinder to success in life. The 13D's, 13F's and 13P's of success are sure keys to God's treasure chest of abundance.
Do yourself good by walking with the principles presented in this book, and you will bid farewell to failure and welcome to success.

Keys To Total Recovery

There are certain things in life that cannot be replaced they have to be recovered. Peter Amenkhienen has packaged together, tested and proven keys to help you recover what the enemy has stolen from you. With the principles in this book, you will become a specimen of the best God can accomplish in human life. The application of these keys will make room for you to move to the next level.

Overcoming The Problems Of Life

Overcoming The Problems Of Life, will help you guide through life with ease, stand tall in spite of the vicissitudes of life, and experience all-round victory. It is time to quit struggling in life. This book will help you overcome discouragement, delay, demons, frustration, failure, fear, the storms of life and poverty as it grants you insight into living the overcoming life.